ARLINGTON NATIONAL CEMETERY

Produce the urn that Hannibal
  contains,
And weigh the mighty dust
  which yet remains:
And is that all?

  — Juvenal

By the same author

FIVE DOWN AND GLORY
JOURNEY OF THE GIANTS
THE WAR IN THE AIR
AMERICANS INTO ORBIT
TEST PILOTS
THE B-29 — THE PLANE
  THAT WON THE WAR
GREAT AIR BATTLES
THE PENTAGON
THE SMITHSONIAN INSTITUTION

ARLINGTON
NATIONAL CEMETERY

*A Picture Story of America's Most Famous
Burial Grounds from the Civil War to
President John F. Kennedy's Burial*

by

GENE GURNEY

with special photography by

HAROLD WISE

CROWN PUBLISHERS, INC., NEW YORK

Location of famous sites at ARLINGTON NATIONAL CEMETERY

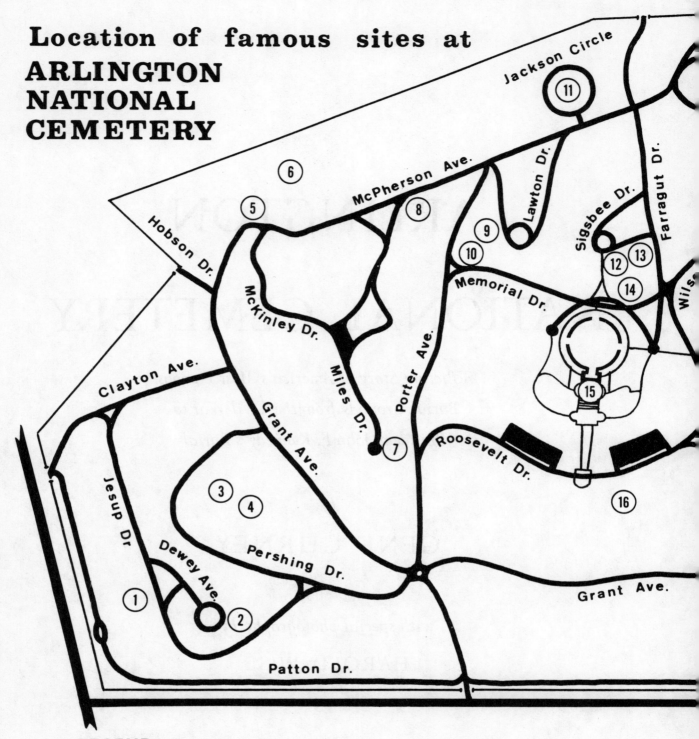

LEGEND
1. ADMIRAL ROBERT E. PEARY
2. WILLIAM JENNINGS BRYAN
3. IRA HAYES
4. GENERAL JOHN G. PERSHING
5. SERGEANT EDWARD F. YOUNGER
6. ARGONNE CROSS
7. WALTER REED
8. ROUGH RIDERS' MEMORIAL
9. JOHN FOSTER DULLES
10. ARMY AND NAVY NURSES MEMORIAL
11. CONFEDERATE MEMORIAL
12. MAST OF THE BATTLESHIP *Maine*
13. IGNACE JAN PADEREWSKI
14. CANADIAN MONUMENT

© 1965, by Gene Gurney. Library of Congress Catalog Card Number: 65-21987 Printed in the U.S.A.

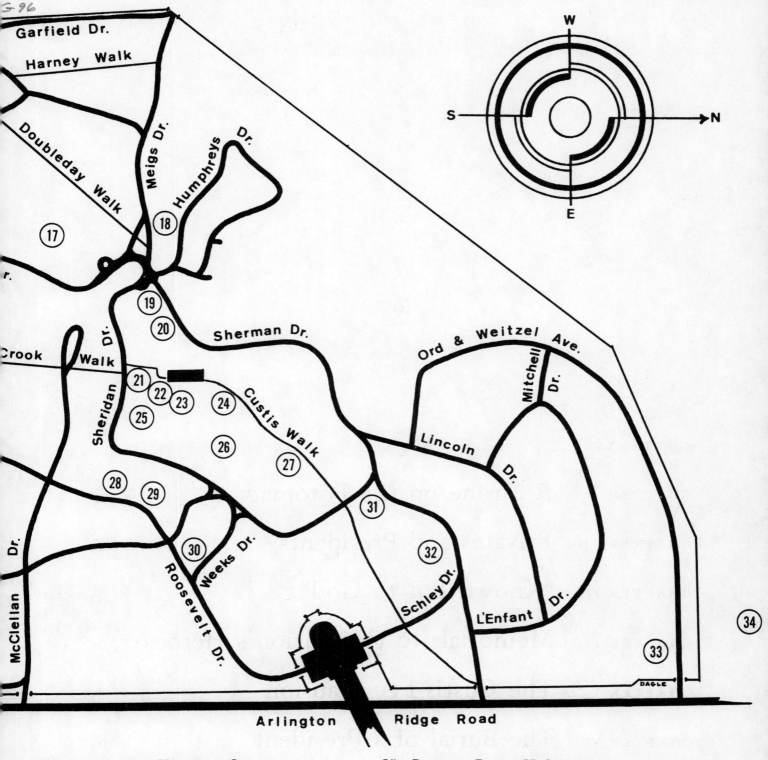

15. TOMB OF THE UNKNOWN SOLDIER
16. GENERAL GEORGE C. MARSHALL
17. CUSTIS BURIAL PLOT
18. ABNER DOUBLEDAY
19. GENERAL PHILIP KEARNY
20. TEMPLE OF FAME
21. GENERAL GEORGE CROOK
22. JOHN CLEM
23. PIERRE CHARLES L'ENFANT
24. MARY MEADE RANDOLPH

25. GENERAL PHILIP H. SHERIDAN
26. PRESIDENT JOHN F. KENNEDY
27. OLIVER WENDELL HOLMES
28. ADMIRAL MARC MITSCHER
29. WILLIAM FRANK KNOX
30. SIR JOHN DILL
31. ROBERT TODD LINCOLN
32. PRESIDENT WILLIAM H. TAFT
33. PRIVATE WILLIAM CHRISTMAN
34. THE NETHERLANDS CARILLON

CONTENTS

I

A Shrine on the Potomac

Arlington National Cemetery, with its monuments and memorials commemorating the dead of every conflict in which the United States has engaged since the Revolutionary War, is one of the nation's most revered shrines. Each year thousands of Americans visit Arlington to see the Tomb of the Unknown Soldier, the grave of President John F. Kennedy, and monuments honoring thousands of others, some of them famous, some unknown.

Located on a wooded hillside across the Potomac River from Washington, D.C., Arlington is one of 85 national cemeteries in the 50 states and Puerto Rico administered by the Department of the Army. Members of the armed services and veterans whose last separation from active duty was honorable may be buried at Arlington or one of the other national cemeteries, and members of their immediate families —spouse, widow or widower, and minor children— may be buried there as well. The United States Government also maintains military cemeteries in Europe, North Africa, and in the Philippines for the dead of World War I and World War II who received permanent burial overseas.

The national cemetery system of the United States, which is more extensive than that of any other country, had its beginning in the days of frontier fighting when military commanders were responsible for the burial of those who died while on duty at outlying forts and posts. Early in the Civil War the Federal Government assumed the responsibility of providing a decent burial for its dead soldiers when President Lincoln was authorized by Congress "to purchase cemetery grounds and cause them to be securely enclosed, to be used as a national cemetery for the soldiers who shall die in the service of the country." The first such cemeteries were established at Alexandria, Virginia, and on the grounds of the Soldiers' Home in Washington, D.C.

The Civil War casualty rate was high, totaling 617,000 dead and 375,000 wounded. In 1864, after three years of fighting, the hospitals and cemeteries in and near Washington were crowded with the injured and dead from Bull Run, Chantilly, and other Virginia battlefields. In many cases the dead were buried without ceremony where they fell, often after they had lain on the battlefield for days, a state of affairs that drew sharp criticism from several influential newspapers. Distressed by the situation, President Lincoln asked his Secretary of War, Edwin M. Stanton, to do something about it. Stanton, in turn, directed the Army Quartermaster General, Montgomery Miegs, to look for a suitable cemetery site in the Washington area.

General Miegs immediately suggested a location—

the Arlington estate owned by the wife of Robert E. Lee, the commander of the Confederate forces who had resigned his commission in the United States Army to fight for the South. At one time Miegs was a friend and admirer of Lee, but he considered Lee's decision to serve with the South an act of treason. Perhaps for that reason the Lee property was the only site Miegs recommended for the new military cemetery.

At the outbreak of hostilities in 1861, Union troops had moved across the Potomac River from Washington to occupy the strategically located Lee estate. By 1864, Mrs. Lee, who had fled to Richmond, owed $92.06 in taxes on her former home, a sum she could well afford to pay, but the payment had to be made in person. When she was unable to pass through the Union lines, the tax-delinquent property was sold to the United States "for Government use, for war, military, charitable, and educational purposes." After the war, Mrs. Lee's son, George Washington Custis Lee, claimed the property, and in 1883, following a Supreme Court decision on the claim, the government paid him $150,000 to obtain a clear title to the estate.

Roughly 200 acres of Arlington became a military cemetery in June, 1864, but the need for burial space was so great by then that interments had already begun. During the remaining months of the war and in the years immediately afterward, thousands of Confederate and Union dead from Virginia battlefields and the military hospitals of the region were buried at Arlington; since then, some of the dead from every one of the country's wars have been buried there, including a few soldiers of the Revolutionary War who were moved from other cemeteries.

Two other national cemeteries, Long Island National Cemetery at Farmingdale, New York, and Golden Gate National Cemetery at San Bruno, California, rank ahead of Arlington in the number of interments made each year, but Arlington's growth has been rapid. In 1930 there were 40,000 graves at Arlington. After World War II the number rose to 85,000, and at the end of 1964 it was 127,000. At the present rate of growth, all available space in the present 420-acre cemetery will be used by 1968. Plans have been made for the eventual addition of another 190 acres because the number of interments at Arlington National Cemetery is expected to increase with the passing years.

Soldiers from every United States war and conflict since the American Revolution lie buried on the wooded slopes of Arlington National Cemetery. The Memorial Amphitheater in the center background commemorates the nation's defenders.

Memorial Bridge, famous for its gold equestrian statues, connects the city of Washington with Arlington National Cemetery across the Potomac River. In the background are Arlington's Memorial Gate and the Custis-Lee mansion.

Memorial Gate is the main entrance to Arlington, but the 420-acre cemetery has several other gates.

Because of its strategic location, the Lee estate was occupied by Federal troops in 1861. In this picture by Civil War photographer Mathew Brady, General Irvin McDowell, who commanded a corps of the Army of the Potomac, and his staff stand on the steps of the Lee house, used as a military headquarters throughout the war.

Located on a hill above the Potomac River, the site of Arlington National Cemetery was once a private estate belonging to the wife of Confederate General Robert E. Lee. The city of Washington can be seen across the river in this picture of Arlington taken at the turn of the century.

Two hundred acres of Arlington officially became a national cemetery on June 12, 1864. By then the mounting numbers of Civil War dead had filled the existing cemeteries in and around Washington, and military burials had already begun at Arlington. The first grave was that of Private William Christman of Company G, 67th Pennsylvania Infantry, located near the present Ord and Weitzel Gate.

Arlington received its first unknown soldier in May, 1864. Headstones with rounded tops were used to mark the graves of the Union dead.

Many of Arlington's Civil War civilian dead were former slaves who sought refuge with Federal troops.

Headstones marking Confederate graves have peaked tops "to keep Yankees from sitting on them."

This photograph taken during the Civil War period shows how rapidly Arlington became a large cemetery. The dead came from the battlefields of Virginia, Army hospitals in the Washington area, and small, abandoned military cemeteries.

Today a Civil War cannon stands on a hill above the rows of Union graves.

John Clem, the youngest soldier of the Civil War, is buried at Arlington. The "Drummer Boy of Chickamauga" joined the Union Army at the age of ten and later served in three more wars. The pillared structure in the background is the Temple of Fame.

John Clem in a picture taken when he was an eleven-year-old soldier in the Union Army. Clem was promoted to sergeant when he was twelve.

7

Arlington's Sheridan Gate, named for Philip Henry Sheridan, the Civil War general, is reserved for pedestrian use.

General Philip Kearny, who lost an arm while fighting in Mexico in 1846, rode into the Confederate lines and was killed by a rifle ball early in the Civil War. General Lee ordered his body returned to Federal forces under a flag of truce.

Abner Doubleday, the inventor of the game of baseball, also won fame as a Civil War soldier. He fired the first gun for the North at Fort Sumter and commanded divisions at the battles of Antietam, Fredericksburg, and Gettysburg.

Doubleday Walk leads to Abner Doubleday's Arlington grave.

A century after the Civil War, over 120,000 headstones in seemingly endless rows mark the graves in what has become one of the largest of the 85 national cemeteries.

The Pentagon, the huge building that houses the Department of Defense, overlooks a corner of Arlington where the soldiers of another day lie buried.

Many of Arlington's tree-covered hills have a parklike appearance.

Each section of graves is numbered and marked.

Always one of America's most beloved shrines, Arlington has been visited by additional millions since the burial there of John F. Kennedy, the 35th President of the United States, who was assassinated in Dallas, Texas, on November 22, 1963. Visitors during 1964 totaled eight million.

PLEASE ACT WITH PROPRIETY HERE AS ELSEWHERE IN THIS CEMETERY IN ORDER THAT OUR DEAD BE PROPERLY HONORED

Cars may be driven into the cemetery grounds through the Treasury, Ord and Weitzel, and Fort Myer Chapel gates. There are several parking areas in the cemetery and others near the main gate. This is the Ord and Weitzel Gate, named for two Civil War generals, Edward Ord and Godfrey Weitzel.

Arlington has ten miles of paved roads.

In the older sections of Arlington, grave markers, many of them privately furnished, vary greatly in size and design. Today privately furnished markers must meet certain specifications, and they are permitted only in those sections where nonstandard markers already exist. In the sections opened since 1947, all graves are marked with regulation headstones furnished and erected by the government.

Either the Cross or the Star of David can be requested for government-furnished headstones.

Close relatives of servicemen or honorably discharged veterans may also be buried at Arlington. To conserve space, all family members are interred in the same grave at different levels.

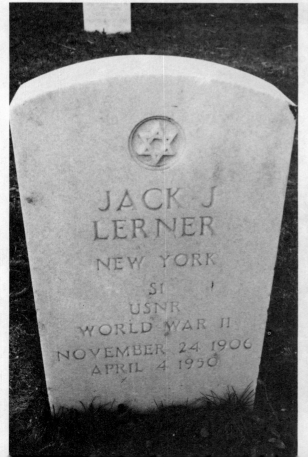

Arlington National Cemetery is administered by a civilian superintendent under the general supervision of the Army's Chief of Support Services.

The superintendent lives in this house on the western edge of the cemetery grounds.

Cemetery offices are located in a special administrative area between Sections 1 and 29.

Machines are used whenever possible. This one disposes of Arlington's mountains of leaves.

Arlington's civilian work force of over 100 men is kept busy the year around.

When the superintendent's office receives a request for Arlington burial (usually from the local undertaker), the deceased's service record is checked by teletype. Requests are normally answered within 48 hours.

Two visitors to Arlington inquire at the cemetery office about the grave of a relative.

Careful records are kept of all Arlington burials.

A member of the Arlington staff traces the route to a grave on a map of the cemetery.

Some families make regular pilgrimages to Arlington to visit the graves of relatives or friends. Flowers and wreaths may be placed on graves at any time. Cemetery officials decorate all graves with small flags for Memorial Day. Flags are not allowed at any other time.

ARLINGTON NATIONAL CEMETERY

This cemetery is situated on the south side of the Potomac River in the State of Virginia, just opposite the City of Washington, D.C. The cemetery was established in 1864 and is administered by the Department of the Army, Office of the Chief of Support Services and under the immediate supervision of the Commanding General, Military District of Washington.

May 1964

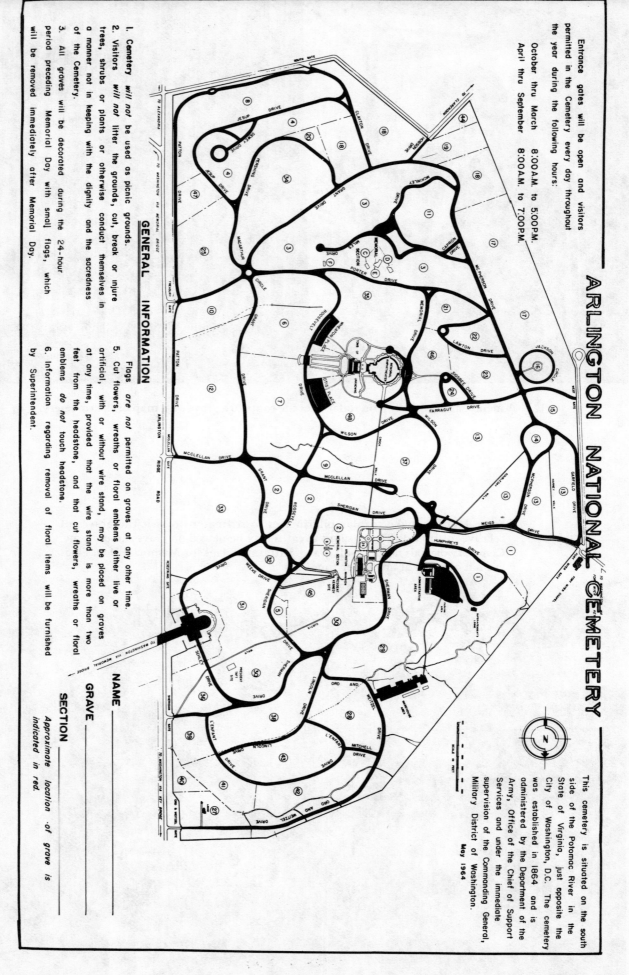

Entrance gates will be open and visitors permitted in the Cemetery every day throughout the year during the following hours:

October thru March   8:00A.M. to 5:00P.M.
April thru September   8:00A.M. to 7:00P.M.

GENERAL INFORMATION

1. Cemetery *will not* be used as picnic grounds.

2. Visitors *will not* litter the grounds, cut, break or injure trees, shrubs or plants or otherwise conduct themselves in a manner not in keeping with the dignity and the sacredness of the Cemetery.

3. All graves will be decorated during the 24-hour period preceding Memorial Day with small flags, which will be removed immediately after Memorial Day.

4. Flags *are not* permitted on graves at any other time.

5. Cut flowers, wreaths or floral emblems either live or artificial, with or without wire stand, may be placed on graves at any time, provided that the wire stand is more than two feet from the headstone, and that cut flowers, wreaths or floral emblems *do not* touch headstone.

6. Information regarding removal of floral items will be furnished by Superintendent.

NAME _____

GRAVE _____

SECTION _____

Approximate location of grave is indicated in red.

This map, with the approximate location and route marked, is given to those who request help in locating a grave.

II

Privates and Presidents

The dignified pageantry of a military funeral takes various forms, the most elaborate of which is the state funeral for a President, a former President, a President-elect, and other persons designated by the President. Burial with full military honors is accorded commissioned officers of the armed services, active or honorably discharged. It includes color-bearers, body-bearers, a caisson, an escort, band, firing party, and bugler. Burial with simple military honors is available to all other military personnel and to commissioned officers for whom it is requested. Simple military honors consist of a bearer party, a firing party, a bugler, and an escorting senior noncommissioned officer. Every military funeral commemorates faithful and honorable service to the United States, and reflects the appreciation of a grateful nation for that service.

Many of the details of a military funeral date back to much earlier times. The use of a caisson probably began during the reign of King Henry VIII when a heavy artillery wagon was used to carry the dead from the battlefield to the burial ground. A battlefield truce, declared to enable the opposing armies to pick up the bodies of their dead for burial and ended by the firing of three rifle volleys, may have been the forerunner of the volleys fired over the grave. The caparisoned, riderless horse carrying a pair of cavalry boots reversed in the stirrups, which is sometimes included in the funeral procession of a general officer or a commissioned officer whose career included mounted service, goes back to the ancient custom of burying a warrior's horse with him. The reversed boots symbolize the fact that the fallen warrior will ride no more.

Many other elements of the funeral—the slow, measured pace of the cortege, the somber music and the muffled drums—exemplify the reversal of the normal order of things. Finally, the poignant bugle call sounded at the conclusion of a military burial service is taps, the last bugle call the serviceman hears at night. It is sounded at the grave to mark the beginning of the last long sleep of those who have served their nation well.

When a request for burial is received at Arlington and the service record of the deceased has been verified, the cemetery superintendent, if requested to do so, will make the necessary arrangements for a military funeral consistent with the rank of the deceased and the wishes of the family. The commander of the Military District of Washington has overall responsibility for military funerals at Arlington. Normally, each branch of the Armed Forces conducts the full and simple honors ceremonies for its own members. If an honor guard is not requested from one of the services, the Army's special Honor Guard carries out all honors.

The flag of the United States covers the casket during every military burial at Arlington. When the graveside committal services are concluded with three volleys from the firing party and the bugle call of taps, the flag is removed from the casket, held taut by the body-bearers, and then precisely folded into a triangular shape. The folded flag is presented to the next of kin or, if none are present, to the cemetery superintendent or his representative who will send it to them.

Over the years many men who won fame in military service or in later civilian careers have been buried at Arlington. The list includes two Presidents of the United States, John F. Kennedy, the 35th President who is buried in Section 45, and William Howard Taft, the 27th President, in Section 30. The grave of Walter Reed, the Army doctor who discovered that yellow fever is transmitted by a mos-

quito, is in Section 3. General Montgomery Miegs, the man who picked Arlington as the site of a national cemetery, was later buried there along with many other famous generals—Philip H. Sheridan and Philip Kearny of the Civil War, George Crook of the Indian wars, John J. Pershing of World War I, and George Catlett Marshall, Jonathan M. Wainwright, Henry H. Arnold, and Claire Chennault of World War II. The United States Navy is represented by such men as Admiral David Dixon Porter, who fought in the Civil War; Rear Admiral Robert Edwin Peary, the discoverer of the North Pole; Rear Admiral Richard E. Byrd, another noted polar explorer; and admirals William F. Halsey and William D. Leahy of World War II fame.

All of those buried at Arlington, the famous and the unknown alike, have served their country, and in so doing, earned a place in the "Shrine of Each Patriot's Devotion."

After World War II many of those who fell in Europe and in Asia were returned to the United States for burial at Arlington. President Harry S Truman (in group at upper left) attended a ceremony honoring the dead heroes in 1947.

General of the Armies John J. Pershing received a state funeral when he died in 1948. Part of the ceremony took place before the Tomb of the Unknown Soldier.

On September 13, 1960, the 100th anniversary of Pershing's birth, President Dwight D. Eisenhower placed a wreath at his grave. The grave is marked with the standard government-supplied headstone.

Fifty-two caskets containing the unidentifiable remains of 250 men lost when the U.S.S. *Serpens* blew up at Lunga Beach, Guadalcanal, were interred in Arlington in 1949. A special monument carries the names of the 250 in alphabetical order.

Led by a chaplain, body-bearers carry a casket from Fort Myer Chapel after a funeral service.

Participants in a full-honor military funeral prepare to leave the Fort Myer Chapel for an Arlington gravesite.

The military members of the funeral cortege march to the grave.

A riderless horse carrying a pair of cavalry boots reversed in the stirrups is often included in the cortege of a general officer or a commissioned officer whose career included mounted service. This is the funeral of a major general.

At the end of the graveside ceremony the flag that covered the casket is removed by the body-bearers and folded into a triangular shape for presentation to the next of kin.

An aerial view of an interment with simple military honors. Simple honors for non-commissioned personnel include a burial party to carry the casket from the hearse to the grave, a six-man firing party, and a bugler to sound taps at the close of the committal service. Simple honors may also be requested for commissioned officers.

JOHN F. KENNEDY
GRAVESITE

The grave of John F. Kennedy, one of the two Presidents of the United States buried at Arlington National Cemetery, is in Section 45.

A tall monument in Section 30 marks the grave of William Howard Taft, the 27th President of the United States. He was also a Chief Justice of the Supreme Court and Secretary of War during President Theodore Roosevelt's administration.

Robert Todd Lincoln, the eldest son of President Abraham Lincoln, and at one time a captain in the United States Army, is buried at Arlington.

Mourners at an Arlington grave.

Because of the cost of travel to Arlington from distant parts of the United States, or a lack of survivors, there are sometimes no mourners at the graveside. In such cases the government assumes complete responsibility for burial arrangements from the time Arlington officials pick up the deceased at Washington's Union Station. Funeral services have often already been held in the hometown.

The remains of veterans who have requested burial at Arlington National Cemetery are delivered to the receiving vault on the cemetery grounds. The government allows $250 toward the burial of all honorably discharged veterans, but it does not pay transportation expenses to Arlington or any other national cemetery except in a few special cases.

Arlington burials, which may number 25 or more a day, are conducted according to a schedule. Coffins remain in the receiving vault until the time set for services. If an American flag does not accompany the remains, one is supplied at Arlington. The flag is later delivered to one of the survivors.

A small mortuary is provided for the use of relatives who wish to view the deceased before burial.

An aerial view of Fort Myer Chapel where Arlington funeral services are held.

Flowers for the mortuary and chapel come from Arlington's greenhouse.

Machinery speeds the task of preparing an Arlington grave.

The same machine that digs the graves later fills them up.

Cemetery workers smooth a newly closed grave with rake and shovel.

Flowers from the funeral are placed on a grave after an interment, an example of the care given the country's honored dead at Arlington National Cemetery.

Workmen unload crates holding headstones for graves in one of the newer sections of Arlington Cemetery, where only the regulation headstone, furnished and erected at government expense, may be used.

Pierre L'Enfant, the man who designed the basic plan for the city of Washington, was reburied at Arlington in 1909, 84 years after his death. L'Enfant served with the American forces during the Revolutionary War.

L'Enfant's plan for Washington is carved on the top of the monument Congress had erected to mark his grave.

The grave of Pierre L'Enfant, marked by a granite slab on six granite legs, overlooks the city he planned.

Bryan Circle in the southwest corner of Arlington Cemetery is named for William Jennings Bryan.

A Secretary of State and a Member of Congress, William Jennings Bryan was also a presidential candidate in three elections and a colonel in the 3d Nebraska Volunteers during the Spanish-American War.

Field Marshal Sir John Dill died in Washington in 1944 while serving as chief of the British Joint Staff Mission. He is one of the few foreign soldiers buried at Arlington.

JOINT RESOLUTION
RECOGNIZING THE OUTSTANDING SERVICE RENDERED TO THE UNITED NATIONS BY
FIELD MARSHAL SIR JOHN DILL

WHEREAS THE CONGRESS HAVING BEEN INFORMED OF THE DEATH OF FIELD MARSHAL SIR JOHN DILL, IN WASHINGTON, DISTRICT OF COLUMBIA ON NOVEMBER 4, 1944; AND
WHEREAS THE ARLINGTON NATIONAL CEMETERY HAS BEEN CHOSEN AS THE FINAL RESTING PLACE OF THIS DISTINGUISHED SOLDIER; AND
WHEREAS AS THE SENIOR BRITISH REPRESENTATIVE ON THE COMBINED CHIEFS OF STAFF FIELD MARSHAL SIR JOHN DILL BY HIS WISDOM AND DEVOTION TO THE VITAL CAUSE OF BRITISH-AMERICAN MILITARY COOPERATION RENDERED A GREAT SERVICE TO THE UNITED NATIONS: NOW THEREFORE BE IT
RESOLVED BY THE SENATE AND HOUSE OF REPRESENTATIVES OF THE UNITED STATES OF AMERICA IN CONGRESS ASSEMBLED THAT THE OUTSTANDING SERVICE RENDERED TO THE UNITED NATIONS BY FIELD MARSHAL SIR JOHN DILL BE AND HEREBY IS RECOGNIZED BY THE AMERICAN PEOPLE AND THE CONGRESS OF THE UNITED STATES.

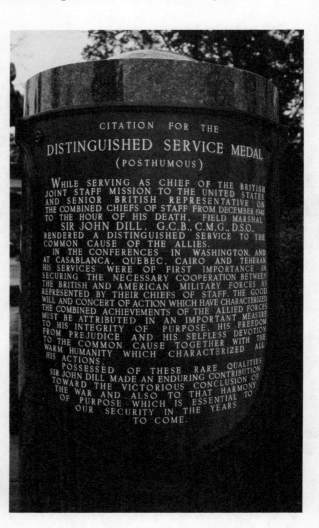

CITATION FOR THE
DISTINGUISHED SERVICE MEDAL
(POSTHUMOUS)

WHILE SERVING AS CHIEF OF THE BRITISH JOINT STAFF MISSION TO THE UNITED STATES AND SENIOR BRITISH REPRESENTATIVE ON THE COMBINED CHIEFS OF STAFF FROM DECEMBER 1941 TO THE HOUR OF HIS DEATH, FIELD MARSHAL SIR JOHN DILL, G.C.B., C.M.G., D.S.O., RENDERED A DISTINGUISHED SERVICE TO THE COMMON CAUSE OF THE ALLIES.
IN THE CONFERENCES IN WASHINGTON, AND AT CASABLANCA, QUEBEC, CAIRO AND TEHERAN HIS SERVICES WERE OF FIRST IMPORTANCE IN SECURING THE NECESSARY COOPERATION BETWEEN THE BRITISH AND AMERICAN MILITARY FORCES AS REPRESENTED BY THEIR CHIEFS OF STAFF. THE GOOD WILL AND CONCERT OF ACTION WHICH HAVE CHARACTERIZED THE COMBINED ACHIEVEMENTS OF THE ALLIED FORCES MUST BE ATTRIBUTED IN AN IMPORTANT MEASURE TO HIS INTEGRITY OF PURPOSE, HIS FREEDOM FROM PREJUDICE AND HIS SELFLESS DEVOTION TO THE COMMON CAUSE TOGETHER WITH THE WARM HUMANITY WHICH CHARACTERIZED ALL HIS ACTIONS.
POSSESSED OF THESE RARE QUALITIES SIR JOHN DILL MADE AN ENDURING CONTRIBUTION TOWARD THE VICTORIOUS CONCLUSION OF THE WAR AND ALSO TO THAT HARMONY OF PURPOSE WHICH IS ESSENTIAL TO OUR SECURITY IN THE YEARS TO COME.

General of the Army George C. Marshall was Chief of Staff during World War II. After the war he served as Secretary of State, Secretary of Defense, and president of the American Red Cross.

Sailors as well as soldiers are buried at Arlington. Admiral Marc Mitscher commanded the famous Task Force 58 in the Pacific during World War II.

Another of Arlington's sailors, Rear Admiral Robert Edwin Peary, led a successful expedition to the North Pole in 1909. His monument was erected by the National Geographic Society.

William Franklin Knox began his military career with the Rough Riders in the Spanish-American War. He later served in World War I and was President Franklin D. Roosevelt's Secretary of the Navy during World War II.

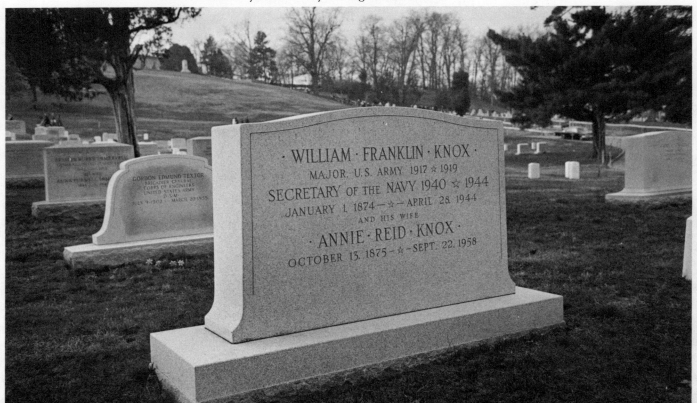

Funeral services for John Foster Dulles, Secretary of State in the Eisenhower Cabinet, were held at Arlington on May 27, 1959. President and Mrs. Eisenhower and Vice-President and Mrs. Nixon are seated in the front row.

Secretary Dulles's tombstone carries his military rank. He was an Army major during World War I.

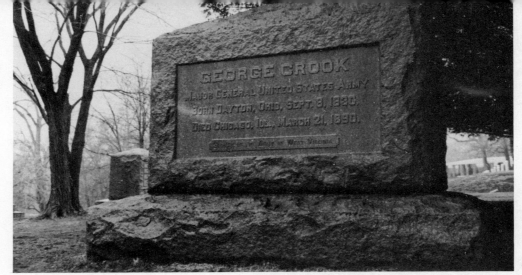

A famous Indian fighter is buried here. General George Crook led units of the United States Army against the Apaches in Arizona and New Mexico, and in 1866 persuaded Apache leader Geronimo to surrender.

On one side of General Crook's tomb is a bas-relief depicting the conference at which his staff and Geronimo's braves discussed surrender terms.

Arlington's Crook Walk, named for General Crook, leads to the Memorial Amphitheater and the Tomb of the Unknown Soldier.

Oliver Wendell Holmes, a veteran of the Civil War and a famous Associate Justice of the Supreme Court, is buried near the grave of President John F. Kennedy. Some of the hundreds of people who visit the Kennedy grave every day can be seen at upper right.

These markers in Section 3 carry the names of servicemen whose bodies were never recovered from airplanes forced down at sea, lost submarines, and similar disasters.

III
"Known But to God"

Probably the best known of all American memorials, the Tomb of the Unknown Soldier has attracted millions of reverent visitors since the burial there in 1921 of an unidentifiable casualty of the First World War. That year, following the lead of its Allies, the United States decided to honor its unknown war dead, and Congress passed a resolution calling for the burial in Arlington National Cemetery of an "unknown and unidentifiable American soldier" who was to be returned from France where 1,648 American unknowns were buried.

The selection process was an elaborate one. First, the body of an unidentified American soldier was removed from each of four World War I cemeteries. The four caskets were taken to the town of Châlons-sur-Marne in northeastern France where six American soldiers waited. On the morning of October 24, 1921, one of the six, Sergeant Edward F. Younger, was chosen to go to the town hall to select the Unknown Soldier from the four unknowns that had been assembled there. All burial records had been destroyed and the four caskets rearranged so that no one knew from which cemetery any one of the four had come.

Sergeant Younger was told to put a rose on one of the caskets to indicate his choice. This is his account of the selection:

"I went into the room and walked past the caskets. I walked around them three times. Suddenly I stopped. It was as though something had pulled me. A voice seemed to say: 'This is a pal of yours.'

"I put the rose on the coffin in front of me and went back into the sunlight. I still remember the awed feeling I had, standing there alone."

That same day the Unknown Soldier began the long journey to Arlington National Cemetery, traveling by train to Le Havre and then on the U.S. cruiser *Olympia* to Washington, D.C. Crowds gathered at Châlons-sur-Marne, at Paris, and at Le Havre to honor the Unknown American Soldier, and more crowds were waiting in Washington where the dead hero lay in state for two days in the Capitol rotunda.

On November 11, Armistice Day, interment ceremonies attended by the great of the nation and representatives of foreign countries were held in the Memorial Amphitheater at Arlington. A stone tomb had been prepared on the amphitheater's east plaza, and there the Unknown Soldier was buried.

The Memorial Amphitheater, built to commemorate the nation's defenders, had been dedicated only the year before, although Congress authorized its construction in 1908 largely as a result of the efforts of the Grand Army of the Republic, a Civil War veterans' organization.

The classic white marble amphitheater carries numerous inscriptions from American history. A quotation from George Washington, "When we assumed the soldier we did not lay aside the citizen," is carved on the wall at the back of the stage. The arch over the stage carries "We here highly resolve that these dead shall not have died in vain" from Lincoln's Gettysburg Address. The piers supporting the arch are inscribed with the names of outstanding Army and Navy commanders from the Revolutionary War through the Spanish-American War. Important battles through the Spanish-American War are listed around the top of the exterior colonnade.

On May 30, 1958, two more symbolic Unknowns

joined the Unknown Soldier of World War I at Arlington. They represented the unidentified dead of World War II and Korea, and they were chosen with the same care as the first Unknown.

The initial steps leading to the return to the United States of a World War II Unknown were taken in 1946 when Congress passed the enabling legislation and the Army began to plan for an interment ceremony to be held on May 30, 1951. Before that date, however, the outbreak of hostilities in Korea caused the project to be postponed. It remained dormant until 1955, when it was revived for Memorial Day, 1958, and enlarged to include an Unknown from Korea as well as one from World War II.

The new plan provided that by mid-May, 1958, two candidates would be selected from among all the World War II unidentified dead buried overseas, one to represent the trans-Atlantic phase of the conflict and the other to represent the trans-Pacific phase. Naval commanders would then assume custody of the candidates, transport them to a place of final selection, choose the World War II Unknown, make disposition of the unselected candidate, and deliver the selectee to Washington. At the same time the Army would select the Unknown of the Korean War and deliver this Unknown to the Navy for transportation to Washington, where the commander of the Military District of Washington would receive the two Unknowns, arrange for them to lie in state in the Capitol, and provide a joint state funeral followed by interment in Arlington National Cemetery on Memorial Day, 1958.

To ensure that all the unidentifiable dead of World War II buried in American cemeteries in Europe and North Africa were properly represented, 13 principals and 13 alternates were designated by lot for disinterment. The 13 principals were exhumed and taken to a mortuary in Frankfurt, Germany, where their caskets were rearranged by successive teams of soldiers to assure their anonymity. With the destruction of all documents, shipping instructions, and identification plates relating to the 13, one of the important phases of the preparatory work was completed.

At the American Cemetery and Memorial in Épinal, France, on May 12, 1958, the 13 unknowns, who had been moved there from Frankfurt, were placed on catafalques beneath a white canopy at the north end of the cemetery's Court of Honor. The caskets, draped with American flags, overlooked a long, grassy mall that terminated at a flagpole on which a flag flew at half-staff. The graves of American military dead flanked the mall on either side.

The selection ceremony began promptly at eleven o'clock. After band music and an invocation, General Edward J. O'Neill, the officer designated to make the selection, moved to a position in front of the row of caskets, saluted, and bowed his head as the chaplain offered a prayer. General O'Neill then walked slowly past the 13 unknowns, pausing in front of each casket. An aide came forward with the selection wreath of red and white carnations, and the general moved slowly to the fifth casket on the left. After placing the wreath in front of the casket, he stepped back, saluted, and left the platform. By eight minutes after eleven the trans-Atlantic candidate-Unknown had been selected.

Meanwhile, in Hawaii, another selection process was under way—for the Unknown to represent the unidentified dead of the trans-Pacific phase of World War II. Here, too, detailed plans had been worked out so that the final choice would be representative of the unidentified of the area, all of whom had been buried either in the National Memorial Cemetery of the Pacific at Honolulu, Hawaii, or in the Fort McKinley American Cemetery and Memorial in the Philippines.

While the candidate-unknowns representing the unidentified dead of World War II were being selected at Épinal and Honolulu, the Army conducted a third selection process to choose the symbolic Unknown to represent the unidentified dead of the Korean conflict, all of whom had been buried in the National Memorial Cemetery of the Pacific.

In due course the U.S.S. *Blandy,* carrying the remains of the Unknown of World War II and the Unknown of Korea, docked at the Naval Gun Factory in Washington, D.C., on May 27. The next morning, with suitable ceremony, the two caskets were moved to the Capitol rotunda, where a large group of Senators and Representatives, the Justices of the Supreme Court, and members of the diplomatic corps joined with the dignitaries who had traveled with the funeral cortege in honoring the two Unknowns.

During the next 48 hours a steady stream of men, women, and children filed past the catafalques in silent homage while private citizens and representatives of organizations left floral tributes at the foot of the caskets. At noon on May 29 the routine was broken for a short period while the caskets were relocated, but the World War II Unknown, as the senior of the two military decedents, remained on the right.

On the afternoon of May 30, Memorial Day, the final pageantry began as body-bearers lifted the caskets from their catafalques and carried them from the rotunda, the World War II Unknown in the lead. Each casket was preceded by a color guard, and a joint honor cordon lined the Capitol steps. While a military band sounded four ruffles and flourishes and played a hymn, the color guards led the way to the black-draped caissons at the foot of the steps, their matched gray teams held in check by riders astride the left horse of each pair. The funeral procession had already formed, and with the arrival of the caskets the march from the Capitol to Arlington National Cemetery began. For the entire distance the streets were lined on both sides by more than 2,000 men of the Army, Navy, Air Force, and Marine Corps standing ten paces apart at parade rest. The men snapped to attention when the national colors and the caissons approached; after the Vice-President's car had passed, they returned to parade rest.

As the caissons crossed Memorial Bridge over the Potomac, the Air Force offered its own salute to the two Unknowns. With a mighty roar twenty planes flew up the river in the "V of V's" formation. The right wingmen in the formations were not present, signifying the missing buddies to whom tribute was being paid.

The long procession passed through the cemetery's Memorial Gate and wound up Roosevelt and Wilson drives to the Memorial Amphitheater, where President Dwight D. Eisenhower and his party were waiting. At the appointed hour of three o'clock the body-bearers lifted the caskets from the caissons and carried them into the amphitheater, placing the World War II Unknown in front of the President and the Unknown of the Korean conflict in front of the Vice-President.

The funeral service began with the national anthem. After an invocation and a solemn two minutes of silence, President Eisenhower stepped forward between the two caskets and spoke just twenty-six words: "On behalf of a grateful people, I now present Medals of Honor to these two Unknowns who gave their lives for the United States of America." As he laid small black pillows on the foot of each casket, the blue ribbons of the nation's highest tribute, the only awards given to the Unknowns

during the funeral rites, showed over the corners.

At the conclusion of the services in the amphitheater, the caskets were carried to the east plaza with the President following the Unknown of World War II and the Vice-President following the Unknown of Korea. After the body-bearers had positioned the caskets over two open crypts before the Tomb of the Unknown Soldier of World War I, Armed Forces chaplains, speaking in English, Latin, and Hebrew, intoned the committal rites of the Protestant, Catholic, and Jewish faiths. Then the President placed a wreath of red and white carnations before the tomb as his personal tribute to the Unknown who had slept in Arlington for so many years and to the two newly arrived heroes. At the command "Present arms" a 21-gun salute was fired, followed by three volleys from the firing squad. An Army bugler sounded taps, and as the ceremony came to a close, the body-bearers carefully folded the flags that had covered the caskets and handed them to the President and Vice-President. The nation's chief mourners in turn gave the flags to the superintendent and assistant superintendent of Arlington Cemetery for permanent display among the tributes to the Unknowns in the Memorial Amphitheater's Trophy Room.

As part of the tribute the nation pays to its servicemen who die unknown, the Tomb of the Unknown Soldier is guarded 24 hours a day by specially chosen soldiers who must meet the Army's highest standards for military bearing and ceremonial training. They are members of the Army's famous Old Guard unit, the 1st Battalion (Reinforced), 3d Infantry, stationed at Fort Myer, the Army post adjacent to Arlington National Cemetery. In addition to providing the men who guard the tomb, the 1st Battalion supplies the soldiers who render military honors at Arlington funerals, and it has ceremonial, security, and alert missions in the Washington area as well.

The Tomb of the Unknown Soldier was first guarded, on a part-time basis, in 1926. Since 1937 it has been under constant guard, day and night, in good weather and bad. While on duty at the tomb, a guard walks his post at a regulation 120 steps per minute. He may not speak or alter his strict military bearing except under extreme circumstances.

The hourly ceremony of the changing of the guard at the Tomb of the Unknown Soldier, attracts many visitors to Arlington National Cemetery.

The imposing white marble Memorial Amphitheater covers 1½ acres in the middle of Arlington National Cemetery. Its center section seats over 4,000 people.

The basement of the Memorial Amphitheater's east pavilion contains a vaulted chapel. In September, 1946, the bodies of five United States airmen shot down over Yugoslavia lay in state there before burial.

One of America's most honored shrines, the Tomb of the Unknown Soldier, is located on the plaza at the east entrance to the Memorial Amphitheater.

The three carved figures on the tomb represent Victory through Valor attaining Peace. The opposite side bears the famous inscription "Here Rests in Honored Glory an American Soldier Known But to God."

Awards made to the Unknown Soldier by the United States Government, foreign countries, and various organizations are displayed in a Trophy Room in the east pavilion of the amphitheater.

The nation's highest award, the Medal of Honor (left), and the Croix de Guerre of Belgium were presented to the Unknown American of the Korean War. The folded flag at the top of the case covered the coffin during ceremonies in his honor.

Chief Plenty Coos of the Crow Nation placed this war bonnet and coupstick on the Tomb of the Unknown Soldier in memory of his tribesmen who died in France during World War I.

A tribute from France in memory of the Americans who fought and died there in 1917 and 1918.

Some of the awards given the Unknown Soldier by American fraternal and civic organizations.

On November 11, 1921, the Unknown Soldier of World War I was buried at Arlington after services in the amphitheater. This picture shows President Warren G. Harding placing the Medal of Honor on the casket.

Sergeant Edward F. Younger, who selected the Unknown Soldier from four unidentified American dead of World War I.

Sergeant Younger was eventually buried at Arlington himself. His grave is in Section 18.

One of the four unknown dead of World War I arrives at the Châlons-sur-Marne town hall, where the final selection took place on October 24, 1921.

An honor guard of French and American soldiers at the bier of the Unknown Soldier at Châlons-sur-Marne.

Units of the French and United States armies and citizens of Châlons-sur-Marne filled the square in front of the town hall as the Unknown Soldier began the journey that would end at Arlington National Cemetery.

The French Government furnished a special railway carriage to transport the Unknown Soldier to the port of Le Havre, where the cruiser *Olympia* waited to carry the dead hero to the United States.

Some of the crowds that lined the streets of Le Havre to see the cortege of the American Unknown Soldier.

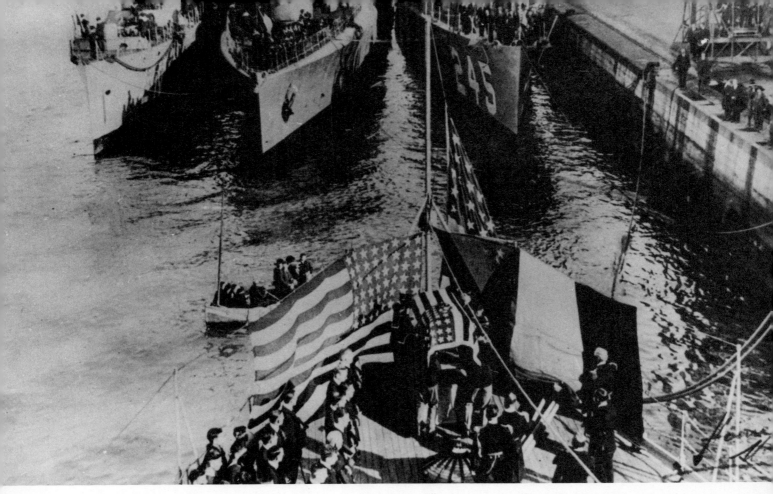

A last ceremony was held on the deck of the *Olympia* before she sailed for the United States.

President Harding places a wreath on the casket of the Unknown Soldier in the **Capitol** rotunda on November 9, 1921.

Former President Woodrow Wilson rides with Mrs. Wilson in the funeral procession that conveyed the Unknown Soldier from the Capitol to Arlington National Cemetery.

An Indian chief pays tribute to the Unknown Soldier. This picture, taken in 1929, shows the plain base and the sub-base that served as the tomb until 1932, when the white marble monument was completed.

Every President since Harding has attended ceremonies at the Tomb of the Unknown Soldier. On November 11, 1939, President Franklin D. Roosevelt stood before the tomb while an Army bugler sounded taps.

President Harry S Truman watches the placing of the traditional wreath on Memorial Day, 1948.

Most foreign dignitaries visit the Tomb of the Unknown Soldier during their stay in Washington. In 1957, Queen Elizabeth and Prince Philip of Great Britain placed a wreath at the tomb while a guard of honor stood at present arms.

By placing a wreath of red and white carnations before one of thirteen caskets, General Edward J. O'Neill selects the Unknown to represent the unidentified United States servicemen who died in Europe and North Africa during World War II.

After the selection ceremony, body-bearers carry the casket of the candidate-Unknown from the memorial at the American cemetery at Épinal, France.

Body-bearers carry the casket to the C-130 aircraft that will take it to Naples, Italy, and the Navy destroyer U.S.S. *Blandy*.

The two unidentified servicemen from the National Memorial Cemetery of the Pacific in Hawaii and the four from the Fort McKinley American Cemetery and Memorial in the Philippines at Hickam Air Force Base prior to the selection ceremony.

Colonel Glenn T. Eagleston places a white carnation lei to indicate his choice of the Unknown to represent the unidentified United States servicemen who died in the western and mid-Pacific areas during World War II.

The honored casket on a special bier during military ceremonies after the selection.

Master Sergeant Ned Lyle, a holder of the Distinguished Service Cross for heroic action in Korea, selects the Unknown of Korea.

Before leaving Hawaii for the United States, the Unknown of Korea lies in state at the National Memorial Cemetery of the Pacific.

The Unknown of World War II and the Unknown of Korea in the Capitol rotunda on May 29, 1958.

Some of the thousands of Americans who lined up to pay tribute to the two Unknowns.

President Dwight D. Eisenhower awarding Medals of Honor to the two Unknowns on behalf of the people of the United States.

The flag-draped caskets of the Unknown of World War II and the Unknown of Korea leave the Capitol for the journey to Arlington National Cemetery. The funeral cortege, which included many military units, was three-quarters of a mile long.

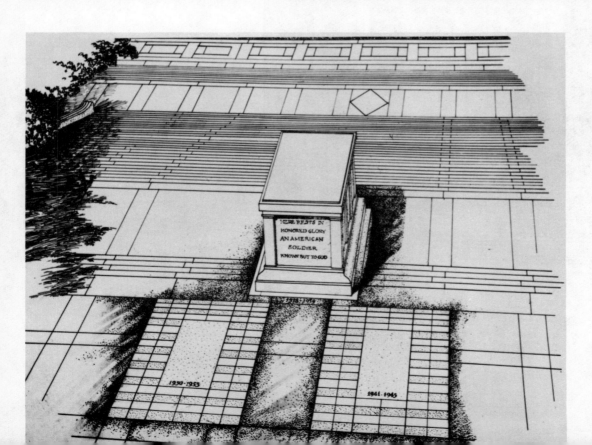

The committal services for the Unknown of World War II and the Unknown of Korea before the Tomb of the Unknown Soldier of World War I on May 30, 1958.

The crypts of the Unknown of World War II and the Unknown of Korea are covered with white marble slabs bearing the dates 1950-1953 for the Korean War and 1941-1945 for World War II.

HERE RESTS IN
HONORED GLORY
AN AMERICAN
SOLDIER
KNOWN BUT TO GOD

1950-1953

1941-1945

From Arlington's Memorial Gate, Roosevelt Avenue leads to the Memorial Amphitheater and the Tomb of the Unknown Soldier.

Carrying his rifle on the shoulder away from the tomb, a traditional way of showing respect for the dead, a guard keeps his silent vigil at the Tomb of the Unknown Soldier.

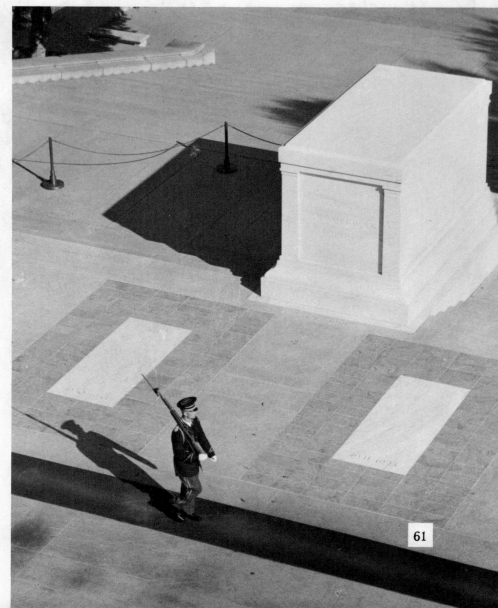

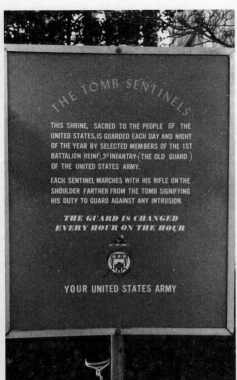

A sign near the tomb explains the sentinel system to visitors.

Sentinels walk their posts in all kinds of weather. *(Photograph by John Full)*

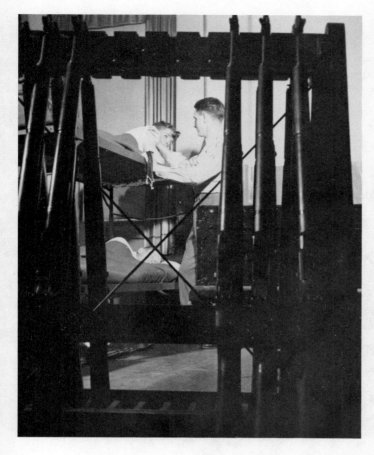

The Old Guard's Company A, whose men stand the 24-hour-a-day watch at the tomb, uses squad rooms located beneath the entrance to the Memorial Amphitheater.

It takes a lot of polishing to get the required shine on scabbard, pouches, and shoes.

Each guard must care for his own clothing and equipment. The blouse (left) is part of the blue dress uniform worn during the winter months.

Rifles have to shine, too. This guard is smoothing his rifle stock with a glass bottle before applying several coats of lacquer. When the job is finished, he will handle his rifle only when wearing gloves, to preserve the luster.

When a soldier guards the tomb, his appearance must be flawless.

Before the ceremony of the changing of the guard, the sentry reporting for duty undergoes a last-minute inspection.

When the ceremony of the changing of the guard begins, the sentinel on post is at the south end of his beat.

On a command from the sergeant in charge of the guard detail, the sentinel marches to the center of the mat, where he is joined by the sergeant and the sentinel reporting for duty.

The two sentinels execute present arms in front of the tomb.

Sentries must be able to execute a perfect present arms, one of several positions they have to master before beginning duty at the tomb.

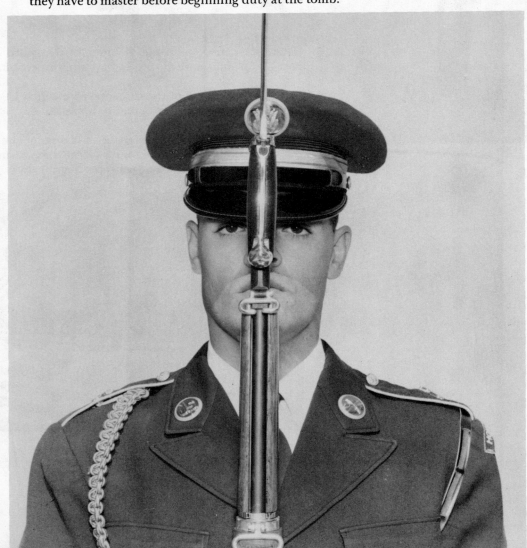

At the end of the ceremony, the sergeant in charge (left) marches the retiring sentinel away from the tomb, and the new sentinel (right) begins walking his post.

At each end of his beat, the sentinel faces the city of Washington for twenty seconds; he then faces the tomb for twenty seconds before resuming his march.

A sergeant of the guards is responsible for the smooth operation of the sentinel system. His eighteen men, who are divided into three groups, or reliefs, also participate in wreath-laying ceremonies at the tomb. Here, the sergeant goes over the ceremony schedule with a corporal in charge of one of the reliefs.

Members of Old Guard units are stationed throughout Arlington National Cemetery to direct traffic and assist visitors. This pair is at the cemetery's West Gate.

The Old Guard's Caisson Section cares for the horses used in full-honor military funerals. Most famous of the Arlington horses is "Black Jack," often used as the riderless, caparisoned horse in the funeral cortege of general officers and those officers whose military career included mounted service. In this picture "Black Jack" carries the traditional black bridle and saddle, sword, and reversed, silver-spurred cavalry boots.

Because the Old Guard has a proud history dating back to 1784, some of its men wear Continental Army uniforms on ceremonial occasions. This is a color guard dressed in "Colonials."

The Caisson Section's brougham is used in Army retirement ceremonies for the traditional farewell ride. And a wedding at the Fort Myer Chapel includes a ride for the bride and groom in the brougham, or "marriage buggy."

IV

Memorials to the Nation's Heroes

The Tomb of the Unknown Soldier is only one of many Arlington memorials commemorating the nation's dead heroes. One of the oldest is the Temple of Fame, a round-domed arbor erected in 1885 by the Grand Army of the Republic, the Civil War veterans' organization. It honors Presidents Washington and Lincoln and ten Civil War generals. The Daughters of the Confederacy erected another of Arlington's Civil War memorials. Located in the center of Jackson Circle, the tall bronze Confederate Memorial is surrounded by concentric rows of Confederate dead who were moved there from an older part of the cemetery in 1901. The memorial was erected in 1914.

The Civil War has its own Tomb of the Unknown Dead, a granite cenotaph above a single grave in which 2,111 unknown Union soldiers killed at Bull Run and on the route to Rappahannock were buried.

Several memorials commemorate the dead of the Spanish-American War. A tall granite shaft west of the Memorial Amphitheater honors all those who fell in Cuba, Puerto Rico, and the Philippines. Nearby is a granite monument dedicated to the Rough Riders, Theodore Roosevelt's famous cavalry regiment. The Army nurses who died in that war have their own monument, erected by the Society of Spanish-American War Nurses.

One of the most unusual of Arlington's monuments honors still another group of Spanish-American War dead—the 253 men who lost their lives in the explosion of the battleship *Maine* in the harbor at Havana, Cuba, on February 15, 1898, an event that led to the war with Spain. The Maine Memorial is the actual mast of the battleship. In 1912, the mast, with its conning tower, was brought to Arlington where many of the *Maine* dead had been buried.

In the southwestern part of the cemetery, in an area occupied by row after row of World War I dead, stands the Argonne Cross dedicated to the American soldiers of that war buried in France. Another memorial erected to the dead of World War I is the Canadian Monument honoring the Americans who died while serving with Canadian forces. Later the inscription on the monument was changed to include those Americans who died while serving with Canadian forces during World War II and the Korean conflict.

In Section 21 a symbolic figure carved from Tennessee marble honors the women buried nearby who served their country as Armed Forces nurses, and in Section 4 a monument has been erected to the men of the Coast Guard who were lost from the *Seneca* and *Tampa* during World War I.

The famous Marine Corps, or Iwo Jima, Memorial is located just outside Arlington Cemetery. Dedicated to all Marines who have given their lives for their country, the memorial depicts the historic flag-raising on Iwo Jima by a detachment of Marines who had won control of the island after a bitter struggle with the Japanese during World War II.

Marines in dress uniform raise the flag on the memorial each morning and lower it in the evening. At night the memorial is floodlighted. The memorial and the 7½-acre tract around it are maintained by the National Park Service.

Arlington's Temple of Fame honors Washington, Lincoln, and ten Civil War generals whose names are inscribed on its eight columns and cornice. The house in the background is the Custis-Lee mansion.

Symbolizing the South at peace, the bronze figure at the top of the Confederate Memorial looks out over Arlington's Jackson Circle. The circular frieze at the base portrays the women of the South sending their men to fight for the Confederacy.

Graves of 400 southern soldiers who fell near Washington surround the Confederate Memorial.

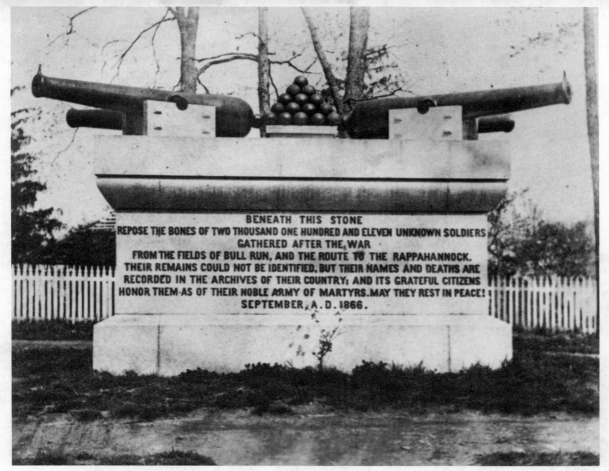

In 1866, 2,111 unknown dead of the Civil War were buried in a vault beneath an elaborate memorial near the Custis-Lee mansion.

Today, the memorial to the unknown dead of the Civil War looks like this. Behind it is another Civil War memorial, the Temple of Fame.

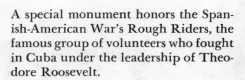

A special monument honors the Spanish-American War's Rough Riders, the famous group of volunteers who fought in Cuba under the leadership of Theodore Roosevelt.

The Spanish-American War Memorial, a tall granite shaft surmounted by an eagle, stands in the center of the area near Lawton Drive where 600 soldiers who died in Cuba, Puerto Rico, and the Philippines are buried. The graves have been decorated with flags for Memorial Day.

Army nurses who died during the Spanish-American War are buried in a plot marked by this memorial.

Rough Riders who died in action are buried around their monument, which is located near McPherson Drive.

The Maine Memorial commemorates the 253 men who lost their lives in the explosion of the battleship *Maine* in the harbor at Havana, Cuba, on February 15, 1898.

A large anchor of the type used by the *Maine* is part of the memorial.

In 1908, some of the casualties of the *Maine* explosion were brought to Arlington for burial in a plot north of the Maine Monument.

Some of the 229 grave markers near the Maine Memorial carry no names because 167 of the victims could not be identified. The names of all those who lost their lives on the ship are inscribed on the memorial.

Ignace Jan Paderewski, the Polish statesman and musician who died in the United States in 1941, is buried in the vault of the Maine Memorial because, first World War II, and since then, the political situation in Poland, have prevented the return of his body to his native land.

In August, 1944, the body of Manuel Quezon, President of the Philippines, was placed in the vault of the Maine Memorial until it could be returned to the Philippines for burial after World War II.

The Argonne Cross, in a large section of World War I graves on the southwestern side of Arlington National Cemetery, is dedicated to the soldiers of that war who are buried in France.

Today the Canadian Memorial also honors the Americans who died while serving with Canadian forces during World War II and the Korean conflict.

Arlington's Canadian Memorial, a bronze sword on a tall granite cross, was erected by Canada in memory of the citizens of the United States who died while serving with Canadian forces during World War I. The Maine Memorial is in the background.

The Army and Navy Nurses Memorial is a tall symbolic figure carved from Tennessee marble.

Nurses who served with the Armed Forces are buried near their memorial in Section 21 of the cemetery.

In the southeastern corner of Arlington National Cemetery, a bronze sea gull poised before a stone pyramid honors the dead of the United States Coast Guard.

Most visitors to Arlington also go to see the United States Marine Corps War Memorial and the Netherlands Carillon, both of which are located just outside the cemetery's northern boundary.

Given to the people of the United States by the people of the Netherlands as a token of appreciation for American aid during and after World War II and as a symbol of the friendship between the two countries, the Netherlands Carillon contains 49 bells. Expert carillonneurs perform at evening concerts during the summertime.

The Iwo Jima Statue is the largest work of cast bronze in the world. Its 10-foot-high base carries the names and dates of Marine Corps combat engagements since 1775. This picture was taken during the formal flag-lowering ceremony held at the memorial each Tuesday evening at 7:30 from mid-May to mid-October.

OPPOSITE PAGE

The famous wartime photograph by Joe Rosenthal of the Associated Press on which the Marine Corps Memorial was based. Three of the six men who raised the flag were later killed on Iwo Jima, and a fourth, Ira Hayes (at extreme left), is now buried at Arlington National Cemetery. *(World-Wide photograph)*

V

The Custis-Lee Mansion

The beautiful Custis-Lee mansion, which stands on a hill in the center of Arlington National Cemetery, is a memorial to Robert E. Lee, one of America's great men. The mansion, Lee's home for many years, is closely connected with the early history of the United States. It was built by George Washington Parke Custis, the grandson of Martha Washington and the foster son of George Washington. When Martha Custis married George Washington, she was a widow with two children. Her son, John, died at the close of the Revolutionary War, leaving four children; two of them, Eleanor Parke Custis and George Washington Parke Custis, were adopted by George Washington and raised at Mount Vernon. In 1802, George Washington Parke Custis, then a young man, moved to a 1,100-acre estate left to him by his father. During the next year he built one wing of a dwelling that he planned to call "Arlington House" after the Custis family's ancestral home on Virginia's Eastern Shore. His architect, George Hadfield, who came from England in 1785 to take charge of the building of the Capitol, had designed a classical structure with two identical wings, a two-story central section, and a large portico supported by eight stately white columns.

Although the bricks and the timber for Arlington House came from his estate, Custis lacked the money to complete all the construction at once. In 1804 he built a south wing. After his marriage that year, Custis and his bride lived in the north wing and used the new south wing for entertaining and for office space.

While building his house, Custis was actively engaged in farming his Arlington estate and other lands that he owned. His interest in improving agricultural practices, particularly the breeding of sheep, led to the development of a fine-wool sheep, called "Arlington Improved," that gained wide acceptance.

In 1808, a daughter, Mary, was born to Custis and his wife, and in 1817, after his finances had recovered from the effects of the War of 1812, he finished his house. The completed Arlington House was considered one of the most beautiful residences in the Washington area. With its two wings, it was 140 feet long. The large central portion was divided by a wide central hall with a formal drawing room on one side and a family dining room and a family parlor on the other. The south wing contained a large formal dining room; the north wing had been divided into small rooms. In front, a portico, providing a magnificent view of the Potomac River, ran across the center portion of the house. In the rear, two buildings used as servants' quarters formed a courtyard.

A visitor to Arlington House shortly after it was completed wrote: "A noble looking place, having a portico of stately white columns, which, as the mansion stands high, with a background of dark woods, forms a beautiful object in the landscape."

When Mary, the Custises' only daughter, married Lieutenant Robert E. Lee in 1831, the wedding took place at Arlington. Lee, a West Point graduate, was assigned to duty with the Corps of Engineers, but the young couple managed to spend much time at Arlington, and six of their seven children were born there.

George Washington Parke Custis died in 1857, leaving his Arlington estate to his daughter for her lifetime and then to his eldest grandson and namesake, George Washington Custis Lee. Because affairs at Arlington needed his attention, Robert E. Lee, by then a colonel, took an extended leave from the Army to devote himself, as executor of Mr. Custis' will, to carrying out its bequests and making the Custis farms as productive as possible.

In February, 1860, Lee reported for duty with the Army in Texas as the disagreement between the North and the South approached the crisis stage. His own feelings on the problem facing the United States are expressed in a letter he wrote to General Winfield Scott: "I can anticipate no greater calamity for the country than the dissolution of the Union. . . . Still a union that can only be maintained by swords and bayonets, and in which strife and civil war are to take the place of brotherly love and kindness, has no charms for me. If the Union is dissolved and the Government dispersed, I shall return to my native state and share the miseries of my people and, save in defense, will draw my sword no more."

Texas seceded from the Union in February, 1861, and Lee arrived home a month later to find Virginia about to do the same thing. He had been ordered to report to Washington for a new assignment as commander of the Federal forces in the field, but when Virginia seceded on April 19, Lee, who felt that his first allegiance was to his state, resigned from the Army. Shortly afterward he left Arlington for Richmond, where he organized Virginia's troops for combat. Mrs. Lee fled to Richmond early in May, just before Federal troops occupied Arlington.

Lee, who had a brilliant military mind, became an adviser to the President of the Confederacy, Jefferson Davis, commander of the Army of Northern Virginia, and finally commander of all the Confederate forces. Although he could not overcome the superior resources of the North, his leadership gave hope and fighting spirit to the South and won the steadfast devotion of his men.

After the war, as president of Washington College, Lee devoted himself to helping the South recover from the ravages of defeat. He urged North and South alike to work for a restoration of the Union, and by his own example did much to bring it about.

Always revered by the South, Lee came to be recognized as a great man by the North as well. His home at Arlington attracted an increasing number of visitors in spite of the fact that its rooms, except those used by the cemetery superintendent as an office and for storage of "grave digging" tools, were empty and uncared for. In 1925, Congress authorized the restoration of the house as a national memorial to General Lee. The restoration, directed by the War Department, got under way in 1928. By 1933, the major portion of the work was finished, and the National Park Service took over the operation of the memorial.

Although a century has passed since Robert E. Lee lived at Arlington, careful restoration has made his presence very real there. A visit to his home provides not only a wealth of information about America's past but also an understanding of the man whose character and courage have won him a secure place in history.

"Arlington . . . where my affections and attachments are more
strongly placed than at any other place in the world," wrote
Robert E. Lee in 1854 of the Custis-Lee mansion, now maintained as a memorial to the great Confederate general.

Once the center of a large wooded estate, the Custis-Lee mansion is surrounded by the white grave markers of Arlington National Cemetery.

George Washington Parke Custis, the adopted son of George Washington, built the mansion.

A sketch of "Arlington House" made before the Civil War.

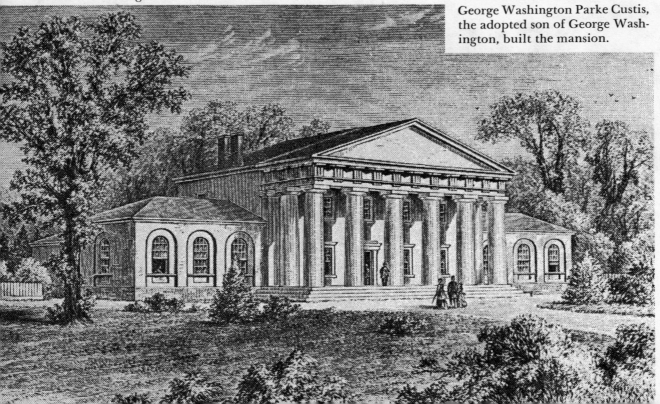

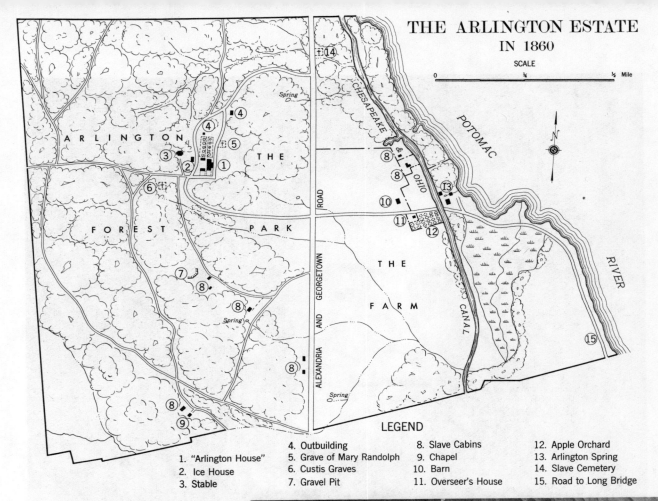

THE ARLINGTON ESTATE
IN 1860

SCALE

LEGEND

1. "Arlington House"	4. Outbuilding	8. Slave Cabins	12. Apple Orchard
2. Ice House	5. Grave of Mary Randolph	9. Chapel	13. Arlington Spring
3. Stable	6. Custis Graves	10. Barn	14. Slave Cemetery
	7. Gravel Pit	11. Overseer's House	15. Road to Long Bridge

Mary, the Custises' only daughter, from a portrait made when she was thirty.

91

Robert E. Lee, from a portrait made in 1838 when he was a lieutenant in the Army.

General Robert E. Lee in 1863, two years after he left Arlington to fight for the Confederacy.

General Lee when he was president of Washington College at Lexington, Virginia, a post he held from the end of the Civil War until his death in 1870. The college was later renamed Washington and Lee University.

After Mrs. Lee left Arlington in May, 1861, her house was used by Federal troops as a headquarters. Some of them can be seen in this photograph taken at the rear of the house.

In the years after the Civil War, admirers of Robert E. Lee visited his old home at Arlington even though its rooms were empty.

The Custis-Lee mansion is one of the national memorials administered by the National Park Service.

The Park Service also cares for the grounds surrounding the mansion.

MEASURED DRAWINGS OF THE MANSION

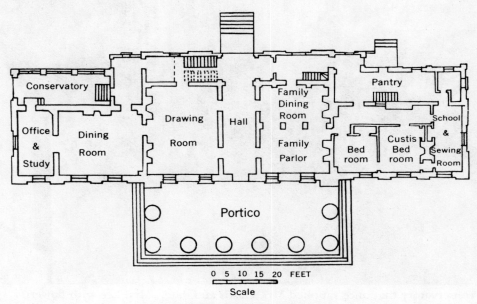

0 5 10 15 20 FEET
Scale

FIRST FLOOR PLAN

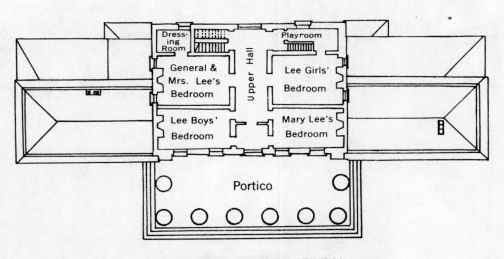

SECOND FLOOR PLAN

The conservatory that once supplied Mrs. Custis and, later, Mrs. Lee with flowers
during the winter months now serves as the entrance to the Custis-Lee mansion.

Mr. Custis and Colonel Lee used this room as an office.

The restored dining room is furnished with chairs that are reproductions of a Sheraton set willed to George Washington Parke Custis by Martha Washington.

A close-up of the elaborate dining-room chandelier.

Unfinished for many years and later used for storage, the drawing room has been restored to look as it did in 1855, the year it was completed. The paintings are copies of the originals.

On special occasions Park Service employees dress in costumes of the pre–Civil War period.

The large hall extending from the
front to the back of the house on the
first floor was used as a summer parlor.

George Washington Parke Custis decorated some of his arched hallways with
elk and deer antlers from the collection
he started when he was a boy at Mount
Vernon.

Each Christmas the family parlor is decorated with a large tree similar to the trees put up by the Custis and Lee families.

Because the original Custis and Lee furniture, silver, and china have been widely scattered over the years, many of the objects now on display in the Custis-Lee mansion are similar pieces obtained through gifts and loans. This china cupboard is in the hall outside the family dining room.

Sofas in the upper hall provided a cool place to sit during Virginia's hot summers.

After the completion of the small and informal family dining room, Mrs. Custis used it instead of the larger dining room in the south wing.

The Lee sons, Custis, Robert, and William, once shared this room.

A corner room on the first floor served as a schoolroom and a sewing room. The globe (right) was discovered in the attic by workmen repairing the roof.

Mary, eldest of the Lee daughters, had a room of her own.

Some of the bedrooms are furnished with the large four-poster beds that were popular in the period before the Civil War. This one is in the room occupied by Colonel and Mrs. Lee.

Before the main part of the house was finished, Mr. and Mrs. Custis used a bedroom in the north wing.

Agnes, Annie, and Mildred Lee shared a large, sunny bedroom.

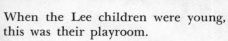

When the Lee children were young, this was their playroom.

The wooden mantelpiece in the Custis bedroom is the oldest in the house.

107

In the wintertime food for the Custis and Lee families and their many guests was prepared in a kitchen under the north wing.

The part of the winter kitchen behind the huge chimney was used as a laundry.

In the summertime a room beneath one of the buildings used as servants' quarters became the kitchen. Though the room was filled in some years before 1861, it has been restored to its original condition.

A tour of the Custis-Lee mansion ends on the lower level of the north wing.

In a room near the exit, the Park Service operates a sales
desk where slides, books, pictures, and souvenirs are sold.

Restoration of the Custis-Lee mansion is a continuous process. As research reveals
information about the house and its outbuildings, and as additional original fur-
nishings are located, rooms and structures are altered to make them closer to the
originals of pre-Civil War days.

This building at the rear of the mansion was known as "Selina's House" because Mrs. Lee's personal maid, Selina Gray, lived in one end of it. A smokehouse and a storeroom occupied the rest of the building.

"Selina's House" has been restored.

Hams and bacon hang from the rafters in the smokehouse just as they did in the days of the Custis and Lee families.

Mary Randolph, believed to have been Mrs. Lee's godmother, was buried a short distance from the Custis-Lee mansion in 1828. Hers is the oldest grave in Arlington National Cemetery.

George Washington Parke Custis and his wife are also buried at Arlington. Their graves, enclosed by an iron fence, are in Section 13 near Doubleday Walk.

One of the first photos taken at Arlington after it became a national cemetery shows the Custis burial plot when a rough wooden fence was being erected around it in June, 1864.

Today, the historic Custis-Lee mansion overlooks the grave of President John F. Kennedy.

VI
The Burial of a President

On November 25, 1963, Arlington National Cemetery was the scene of perhaps the saddest funeral in its 100-year history. On that day, John F. Kennedy, the 35th President of the United States, was brought to Arlington for burial among the nation's heroes.

Felled by an assassin's bullets after only three years in office, the dead President left behind him plans and aspirations as yet unrealized, but during his brief tenure as Chief of State he had stirred the imagination of the world and won the admiration of millions.

From all over the world, emperors, kings, presi-dents, and prime ministers came to Washington, where they joined with the humble and the great of the United States in mourning for the dead President.

The afternoon shadows were already lengthen-ing on Monday, November 25, when President Kennedy was brought at last to the Arlington hillside where he would lie among the nation's honored dead. As darkness fell and thousands stood in line to pass before the grave, the eternal flame was burning for the man who had cast such a bright light for such a short time.

The 35th President of the United States, John Fitzgerald Kennedy, with Mrs. Kennedy and their children, John, Jr., and Caroline, at Palm Beach, Florida, in the spring of 1963. *(Photo by Cecil Stoughton)*

Surrounded by a guard of honor from the Army, Navy, Air Force, Marines, and Coast Guard, the body of President Kennedy lies in repose in the East Room of the White House on November 23. Throughout the day government leaders and foreign representatives filed past the flag-draped coffin that rested on the same catafalque that 98 years earlier had borne the remains of the slain President Abraham Lincoln. *(Photo by Cecil Stoughton)*

On Sunday, November 24, a sad procession bears the body of President Kennedy from the White House to the Capitol, where it would lie in state in the rotunda for 21 hours. Ten cars carrying members of the Kennedy family, President and Mrs. Lyndon Johnson, security agents, and others followed the horse-drawn caisson down Pennsylvania Avenue.

Twenty-four servicemen, 12 on each side, flank the black caisson as it moves down Pennsylvania Avenue. The same caisson carried the body of President Franklin D. Roosevelt from the White House to the Capitol in April, 1945.

The slow throb of muffled drums accompanies the procession.

Followed by the traditional riderless horse carrying cavalry boots reversed in the stirrups and a black-handled sword in a silver scabbard, the caisson with its honor guard enters the East Capitol Plaza where an estimated 35,000 people waited.

Body-bearers from the Army, Navy, Air Force, Marine Corps, and Coast Guard carry the remains of the slain Commander in Chief up the east steps of the Capitol.

Mrs. John F. Kennedy, her children, Caroline and John, Jr., President and Mrs. Johnson, and Attorney General Robert Kennedy watch as the late President returns to the Capitol where he had served as both a Member of the House and as a Senator. *(Photo by Ralph Seghers)*

Holding Caroline and John, Jr., by the hand, Mrs. Kennedy follows the casket up the Capitol steps. Behind her are (from left to right) Attorney General Robert Kennedy, Mr. and Mrs. Stephen Smith, and Mr. and Mrs. Peter Lawford.

An estimated 250,000 people filed past the bier of the slain President while it lay under the Capitol dome in the historic rotunda. At 9:00 A.M. on Monday, November 25, with 12,000 people still in line, the Capitol doors were closed and the body was moved to St. Matthew's Cathedral. *(Photo by Frank Hall)*

Among those watching as the body-bearers removed the presidential casket from the caisson and carried it into the cathedral are former President Dwight D. Eisenhower, President Charles de Gaulle of France, King Baudouin of Belgium, and Emperor Haile Selassie of Ethiopia. Many of the distinguished mourners had followed the caisson on foot from the White House.

At the conclusion of the hour-long Requiem Mass, the eight bearers carry the flag-covered casket from the cathedral.

The nation's military leaders render a hand salute as their late Commander in Chief is borne down the cathedral steps. From the left: General Maxwell Taylor, USA; General Curtis E. LeMay, USAF; General Earle G. Wheeler, USA; Admiral David L. McDonald, USN; General David M. Shoup, USMC; and Admiral Edwin J. Roland, USCG.

Former President Eisenhower walks slowly from the cathedral after the Mass.

123

Heads of state, foreign dignitaries, and members of the diplomatic corps wait outside the cathedral while the slain President's casket is carried back to the caisson.

The body-bearers carefully adjust the flag after placing the casket on the caisson for the journey to Arlington National Cemetery.

Before the arrival of the President's cortege, an Army unit, one of the many that lined the route of the funeral procession, moves into position near the Lincoln Memorial. The Washington Monument is in the background. *(Photo by Carlos Ruis)*

President Kennedy's last journey through the streets of Washington takes him past the Lincoln Memorial. *(Photo by Elmo J. Shingleton)*

Bereted soldiers of the Army's guerrilla-war-trained Special Forces march in the funeral procession. *(Photo by Shackelford)*

Eighty-nine-man companies represented the military academies in the funeral procession.

Cadets from West Point. *(Photo by Shackelford)*

Midshipmen from Annapolis. *(Photo by Elmo J. Shingleton)*

Cadets from the Air Force Academy. *(Photo by Elmo J. Shingleton)*

A long line of cars carrying members of the Kennedy family, government officials, foreign dignitaries, and members of the diplomatic corps follows the caisson from St. Matthew's Cathedral to Arlington National Cemetery. *(Photo by Harold Switzer)*

Silent crowds line the route to Arlington and wait at the cemetery entrance. The Colonial Fife and Drum Corps of the Army's 3rd Infantry (Old Guard) stands at attention (foreground) as the six gray horses enter the cemetery and begin the climb up the winding road to the place where the President will be buried. *(Photo by Harold Switzer)*

Members of the Irish Guard stand at parade rest as the funeral procession approaches the grave. Later, an honor guard of Irish cadets executed a manual of arms for death, a tradition at military funerals in Ireland. President Kennedy had seen and admired the ceremony during his visit to Ireland. *(Photo by Frank Hall)*

As the caisson comes to a halt and the body-bearers remove the casket for the last time, Air Force One, the President's personal plane, flies over the cemetery, dipping its wings in salute.

Preceded by a three-man color guard and members of the clergy, the body-bearers carry the slain President from the caisson to the waiting grave.

Richard Cardinal Cushing, Archbishop of Boston, performs the rites of the Catholic Church during the brief graveside service. *(Photo by Frank Hall)*

While all those in uniform hold a last long salute, the body-bearers begin the folding of the casket flag for presentation to Mrs. Kennedy. *(Photo by Ralph Seghers)*

At the conclusion of the committal service, Mrs. Kennedy ignites the eternal flame that she had requested for her husband's grave.

As the hundreds of somber mourners begin to leave, the
eternal flame burns before the still unlowered casket.

By evening an Army Special Forces green beret has been placed
in tribute beside the eternal flame. *(Photo by John Full)*

The beret is soon joined by other military headgear left at the
eternal flame in silent tribute to the fallen Commander in Chief.

During the first year after President Kennedy's
death, almost eight million people visited his grave.

Some of the millions of visitors to the grave bring floral tributes; all of them come to honor the memory of the dead President.

VII

The Eternal Flame

The eternal flame ignited by Mrs. John F. Kennedy when the late President was buried at Arlington National Cemetery on November 25, 1963, is the central theme of the design for his permanent resting-place. It will burn as a symbol of special public respect at the head of his grave, 20 feet below the place where he was first buried, on the same beautiful Arlington hillside.

The permanent burial site has been planned to accommodate as many as 50,000 visitors a day, while retaining for each visitor a sense of intimacy as he views the grave of the 35th President. The design for the site is the work of architect John Warnecke, who, at Mrs. Kennedy's request, inaugurated the project shortly after the President's death. Mr. Warnecke felt that the design for the gravesite should combine the ideas and feelings of the present with the traditions of the past and at the same time reflect the character of the 35th President. Members and friends of the Kennedy family gave him their suggestions, and he consulted with landscape architects, artists, stonecutters, and other craftsmen. The design that resulted won the approval of the Kennedy family and the various government agencies involved in the project.

Ownership of the 3.4-acre burial site has been retained for the nation as a whole, and not deeded to the Kennedy family, although the area was never intended for burial purposes because of its hilly nature. The Department of Defense, which administers Arlington National Cemetery, plans to complete construction of the gravesite, walkways, platforms, and other improvements in the area by the fall of 1966. At that time President Kennedy's remains will be moved from their temporary resting-place.

Construction costs, estimated at $2 million, will be shared by the government and the Kennedy family. The government will pay for walks and other facilities used by the public, and the family will pay for construction in the area immediately surrounding the grave. The entire site will be maintained by the government as part of Arlington National Cemetery.

Like all Chief Executives, President Kennedy made several visits to Arlington National Cemetery during the three years he was in office. His last visit was 11 days before his death when he placed a wreath at the Tomb of the Unknown Soldier on Veterans Day, 1963. During an earlier visit he had admired the beauty and serenity of Arlington, and remarked, "I could stay here forever." The site chosen for his permanent burial is close to the spot where he stood when he spoke those words, and the eternal flame at his grave will burn high above the city of Washington where he served his country as Member of the House of Representatives, Senator, and President.

Architect John C. Warnecke explains the setting he designed for President Kennedy's permanent grave in Arlington National Cemetery to Eunice Shriver, the late President's sister, and Secretary of Defense Robert S. McNamara. The model shows the details of the gravesite and its approaches. The building at upper left is the Custis-Lee mansion.

A circular walkway will lead to the grave, shown here at top center. Visitors will normally follow the walk that curves around to the right. The shorter walk to the left will be used for official wreath-laying ceremonies.

The grave will be approached from an elliptical terrace designed to serve as an overlook where visitors can spend a few moments in contemplation. The low, tapered wall of the overlook will be inscribed with quotations from the late President's speeches.

The President's grave will lie in a slightly elevated, rectangular grass plot surrounded by a marble terrace. His two deceased children will lie on either side in graves marked by small tablets.

Behind the simple tablet marking President Kennedy's grave, the eternal flame will burn in a three-pronged brass font.

137

A view of President John F. Kennedy's final resting-place in Arlington National Cemetery with the Lincoln Memorial in the background. The Washington Monument and the Capitol are at upper right. The wall in the foreground is the terminal point of the grave design.

VISITING HOURS

Arlington National Cemetery is open from 7:30 A.M. to 7:00 P.M., from April 1 to September 30, and from 7:30 A.M. to 5:00 P.M., from October 1 to March 31. When daylight-saving hours are in effect, the cemetery remains open until 9:00 P.M.

The Custis-Lee mansion is open from 9:30 A.M. to 4:30 P.M., October through March, and from 9:30 A.M. to 6:00 P.M., April through September. There is an admission charge of 50 cents that is waived for children and young people 15 years of age and under and for educational groups.

BUS SERVICE

Bus service is available from Washington D.C. Automobiles may be driven through the cemetery and to the Custis-Lee mansion.